The expert enjoys an edge over the average player in that he knows how to exploit the full potential of the partnership cards. In the play of the hand his experience enables him to marshall the odds in his favour, giving himself not only the obvious chance of making the contract but also those extra chances that so often make the difference between success and failure.

In this book the authors show how it is done, with forty well-chosen examples covering a wide range of standard themes. After absorbing the techniques described in these pages, the reader will find himself making contracts that he could not have hoped to make before.

The authors have won equal distinction as players and as writers on the game. For many years Roger Trézel was an automatic choice for the French International Team, as was Terence Reese for the British.

Both are European and World Champions.

Master Bridge Series
General Editor: Hugh Kelsey

A distinguished new series which contains
books by the world's foremost experts on all
aspects of the game, ranging from books
for beginners to books on advanced
techniques of bidding and play.

Terence Reese and Roger Trézel

Those Extra Chances in Bridge

A World of Books That Fill a Need

Frederick Fell Publishers, Inc.,
New York, N.Y. 10016

First published in Great Britain in 1978
by Ward Lock Limited, 116 Baker Street,
London, WIM 2BB. A member of the Pentos Group.

For information address:
Frederick Fell Publishers, Inc.
386 Park Avenue South
New York, New York 10016

Library of Congress Catalog Card No
77-23675

International Standard Book Number
0-88391-077-2

Published simultaneously in Canada
Thomas Nelson and Sons
Canada (Limited)
81 Curlew Drive
Don Mills, Ontario
M3A 2R1 Canada

Printed and bound in Great Britain
by R. J. Acford Ltd, Chichester, Sussex

Introduction

by Terence Reese

The play of the cards at bridge is a big subject, capable of filling many large books. Some years ago Roger Trézel, the great French player and writer, had the idea of breaking up the game into several books of the present length, each dealing with one of the standard forms of technique. He judged, quite rightly as it turned out, that this scheme would appeal both to comparative beginners, who would be able to learn the game by stages, and to experienced players wishing to extend their knowledge of a particular branch of play.

We have now worked together on an English version, profiting from his experience. The first six titles in the series are:

1   Safety Plays in Bridge
2   Blocking and Unblocking Plays in Bridge
3   Elimination Play in Bridge
4   Snares and Swindles in Bridge
5   Those Extra Chances in Bridge
6   When to Duck—When to Win in Bridge

Other titles are in preparation.

Those Extra Chances

The French title of this book is *Précautions et Soins*, a phrase used in medicine, similar in meaning to the motorist's 'due care and attention'. Some of the examples appear to involve safety plays, but they are not exactly that, for there is no guarantee of success. The problem is to find the line of play that offers the best chance.

There are several examples on standard themes such as suit establishment, technique in finessing, avoiding a dangerous lead, attacking the danger hand, averting a ruff, and many forms of communication play. In every case the right line of play can be determined by logical analysis; the reader is not called upon to perform feats of counting or deduction, nor is a knowledge of end-play demanded. These are the basic techniques with which every aspiring player must be familiar.

Example 1

There is nothing fixed about the timing of a finesse in bridge. On
many hands the declarer will postpone a finesse until the last possible
moment, hoping that somehow it can be avoided. The deal below was
different: quite early in the play the declarer took a finesse which
could not possibly gain a trick in the suit, even if it succeeded. The
finesse was nevertheless necessary because it provided an extra entry
to the dummy.

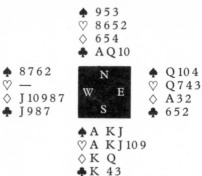

```
                    ♠ 9 5 3
                    ♡ 8 6 5 2
                    ◇ 6 5 4
                    ♣ A Q 10
   ♠ 8 7 6 2                      ♠ Q 10 4
   ♡ —              N             ♡ Q 7 4 3
   ◇ J 10 9 8 7   W   E           ◇ A 3 2
   ♣ J 9 8 7        S             ♣ 6 5 2
                    ♠ A  K J
                    ♡ A  K J 10 9
                    ◇ K  Q
                    ♣ K  4 3
```

North-South reached an optimistic contract of six hearts.

SOUTH	WEST	NORTH	EAST
2 ♣	pass	2 ◇	pass
2 ♡	pass	3 ♡	pass
3 ♠	pass	4 ♣	pass
5 ♡	pass	6 ♡	pass
pass	pass		

South did rather too much. After the negative response of two
diamonds a slam was not very likely, and over four clubs South
should have been content with four hearts, leaving any further move
to his partner.

West led the jack of diamonds, East won with the ace and returned a
diamond to the declarer's king. On the ace of hearts West showed
out, discarding a diamond.

South had been hoping for an even break in hearts, but now it was
evident that he would need two finesses to pick up East's queen.
The ace and queen of clubs would supply entries for this purpose,
but what about the third round of spades ? To drop a doubleton
queen was a slender chance.

The solution was to take an 'unnecessary' finesse of the ten of clubs. When this succeeded, South was able to finesse against the queen of spades as well as against the queen of hearts.

You may think that declarer could begin with a club to the queen, intending to finesse the ten on the next round. But this would give West the chance to make the fine blocking play of the jack of clubs on the second round. Then declarer would be unable to obtain three entries in clubs.

Example 2

Do not allow yourself to be deflected from the right line of play by a danger that is real in one sense, but imaginary in another: imaginary, because if the feared distribution exists, then the contract will be impossible anyway. The theme illustrated below is very common.

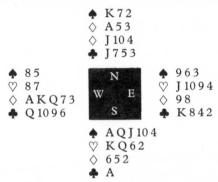

```
                    ♠ K 7 2
                    ♡ A 5 3
                    ◊ J 10 4
                    ♣ J 7 5 3
   ♠ 8 5                         ♠ 9 6 3
   ♡ 8 7            N            ♡ J 10 9 4
   ◊ A K Q 7 3   W     E         ◊ 9 8
   ♣ Q 10 9 6       S            ♣ K 8 4 2
                    ♠ A Q J 10 4
                    ♡ K Q 6 2
                    ◊ 6 5 2
                    ♣ A
```

South was the dealer, with both sides vulnerable, and the bidding went like this:

SOUTH	WEST	NORTH	EAST
1 ♠	pass	1NT	pass
2 ♡	pass	3 ♠	pass
4 ♠	pass	pass	pass

It is rare for a player who has responded one no trump to jump on the next round, but North correctly attached importance to the good cards in each of the suits bid by his partner.

The defence began with three rounds of diamonds. When his partner discarded a low club on the third round, West switched to the eight of hearts, which was won by the declarer's king.

Now, if the hearts are divided 3—3, the hand presents no problem. But a 4—2 break is more likely and the declarer must consider what he can do to overcome that distribution.

The solution is to draw just two rounds of trumps, then play on hearts. It may seem a little dangerous to leave a trump outstanding, but if you study the matter more closely you will see that this line provides an extra chance and no additional risk. If the hearts are 4—2 you are not going to make the contract anyway. But there is a chance that the last trump will be in the same hand as the long heart. As the cards lie, South draws two trumps with the ace and queen, then plays on hearts, ruffing the fourth round with dummy's king of spades.

Since there are always people who write to say 'Your hand is wrong because . . .', we will make a small safety play of our own by adding that there is another line of play that may possibly succeed. Suppose that declarer, ignoring the play we have suggested, cashes ace of clubs, plays three rounds of trumps, finishing in dummy, and ruffs a club. Then he plays off the fifth trump. If East began with K Q of clubs, or any six clubs plus four hearts, he will be squeezed. A good player would note this possibility but would reject it in favour of the play described above.

Example 3

This type of hand is often a source of trouble in the bidding:

♠ K Q 5 2
♡ A 10 9 3 2
♢ 9 3
♣ A Q

You open one heart and partner responds one no trump. Do you then rebid two hearts or two spades or do you pass ? Undoubtedly, the pass is correct, because partner has had an opportunity to respond one spade on a four-card suit and has not done so.

Some players seek to escape the problem by opening with a 'prepared' bid of one spade. The disadvantage of that method is that partner may give preference to spades on the next round and you end up in the wrong trump suit.

When the deal below was played, South not only reversed but bid one more 'for the road'.

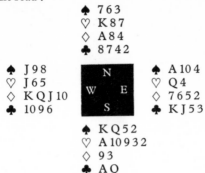

```
                    ♠ 7 6 3
                    ♡ K 8 7
                    ◇ A 8 4
                    ♣ 8 7 4 2
    ♠ J 9 8              N           ♠ A 10 4
    ♡ J 6 5                          ♡ Q 4
    ◇ K Q J 10       W       E       ◇ 7 6 5 2
    ♣ 10 9 6              S          ♣ K J 5 3
                    ♠ K Q 5 2
                    ♡ A 10 9 3 2
                    ◇ 9 3
                    ♣ A Q
```

The bidding went:

SOUTH	WEST	NORTH	EAST
1 ♡	pass	1NT	pass
2 ♠	pass	3 ♡	pass
4 ♡	pass	pass	pass

West led the king of diamonds and obviously prospects were poor. To make the contract, South would need the club finesse and he could afford to lose only one heart and one spade. He had to find East with S A x x, and for the club finesse and two leads up to S K Q x x he would need three entries to the table. Only two were visible—the ace of diamonds and the king of hearts.

South created the extra entry by a manoeuvre similar to that used on Example 1. Having won the first trick with the ace of diamonds, he successfully finessed the queen of clubs, then led the ten of hearts and let it run to East's queen. When the defence played diamonds, South ruffed the third round with the nine of hearts, led a low heart and finessed the eight, which held. He played a spade to the king, entered dummy with the king of hearts, and led another spade to the queen. When the spades broke 3—3 he was able to claim the contract and was, no doubt, proud of his enterprise.

Example 4

While it is usual, as we remarked earlier, to postpone a finesse in a
side suit, there are times when it is clear that the finesse must be
taken some time and there may be advantage in taking it early on.

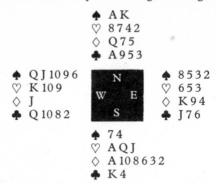

```
                    ♠ A K
                    ♡ 8 7 4 2
                    ◇ Q 7 5
                    ♣ A 9 5 3
    ♠ Q J 10 9 6                      ♠ 8 5 3 2
    ♡ K 10 9         N                ♡ 6 5 3
    ◇ J          W       E            ◇ K 9 4
    ♣ Q 10 8 2        S               ♣ J 7 6
                    ♠ 7 4
                    ♡ A Q J
                    ◇ A 10 8 6 3 2
                    ♣ K 4
```

In contrast to some that we have noted up to now, this hand was
quite well bid:

SOUTH	WEST	NORTH	EAST
—	—	1 ♣	pass
2 ◇ (1)	pass	3 ◇	pass
3 ♡	pass	3 ♠	pass
3NT	pass	4 ♣ (2)	pass
4 ◇	pass	6 ◇	pass
pass	pass		

1) The force is a little old-fashioned, but none the worse for that.
Players seem to have forgotten that a jump is a force to game, not an
invitation to slam.

2) At this point North is showing controls. He is waiting for
confirmation that his partner has a fair suit of diamonds.

To bid a slam with a combined 27 points and no singleton or void is a
good achievement, but South's play was not as commendable as the
bidding. Having won the spade lead in dummy he played ace and
another diamond, this being the best way to avoid two losers in the
suit. He was reasonably lucky in the trump suit, but when the heart
finesse lost he was one down.

What was wrong with the play ? Well, the two red suits must be studied in combination. If the heart finesse is right, then it is right to play the diamonds as South did. But if the heart finesse is wrong, then declarer must play the trump suit to lose no tricks at all. The only chance for this is to lead the queen from dummy, in the hope of pinning a singleton jack in the West hand. (Note that it will not help to drop a singleton king in either hand.)

Since the play in the trump suit depends on the fate of the heart finesse, the declarer's first move should be to test the hearts by finessing the queen at trick two. West (unless he is exceptionally perspicacious) will win with the king. Knowing then that he cannot afford to lose any trick in diamonds, South will broach the suit by leading the queen from dummy. East will probably not cover with the king; if he does, the jack will fall under the ace and South will re-enter dummy to finesse against East's ♢ 9 4.

Example 5

Sometimes it is not at all easy to work out the only distribution of the adverse cards that will provide a chance for the contract. South had a plan of sorts on the deal below, but at best he was depending on a defensive error.

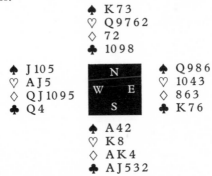

```
                    ♠ K 7 3
                    ♡ Q 9 7 6 2
                    ♢ 7 2
                    ♣ 10 9 8
   ♠ J 10 5                        ♠ Q 9 8 6
   ♡ A J 5              N          ♡ 10 4 3
   ♢ Q J 10 9 5     W     E        ♢ 8 6 3
   ♣ Q 4               S          ♣ K 7 6
                    ♠ A 4 2
                    ♡ K 8
                    ♢ A K 4
                    ♣ A J 5 3 2
```

The bidding did not take long:

SOUTH	WEST	NORTH	EAST
—	—	pass	pass
1♣	1♢	1♡	pass
3NT	pass	pass	pass

North's free bid of one heart, on his moderate values, was very questionable. When West led the queen of diamonds and North had to expose his dummy, he came out with the old bromide, 'Not much, partner, but I had passed originally'.

There was not much point in holding off the first diamond—it might even be a mistake to let the defence switch to spades with a trick in the bag. South won the diamond lead, therefore, and considered his prospects.

There was a reasonable chance to make four tricks in clubs. With two entries to dummy, declarer could take two finesses; with only one entry, he could lead low from hand, playing West for Q x or K x. But four clubs, two diamonds and two spades would add up to only eight tricks. Having concluded that he would need at least one trick from hearts, South led the king of hearts at trick two. He hoped that the defence, seeing the heart suit in dummy, would allow the king to hold.

West captured the ace of hearts at once, however, and cleared the diamonds. Whether he played on hearts or clubs now, South could make only eight tricks.

Since his aim was to slip through just one trick in hearts, South should have thought of leading a *low* heart at trick two.
As it happens, this play confronts the defence with a dilemma to which there is no answer. If West plays low, South wins with the queen in dummy and switches to clubs, establishing four tricks in this suit; if West goes up with the ace of hearts to clear the diamonds, then South can make four tricks in hearts, which also is enough for his contract.

This lead of a low heart has good chances of success even if the hearts are not 3—3. Holding either A x of hearts, or A J x x, West may fail to go up with the ace, not realizing that declarer's intention is to go up with the queen and then abandon the suit.

Example 6

There are various suit combinations where the declarer seems to need just a simple finesse; but when there is a possibility that the critical card may be well guarded, he may need to be careful which card he leads on the first round.

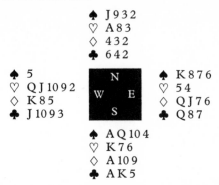

```
                    ♠ J 9 3 2
                    ♡ A 8 3
                    ◇ 4 3 2
                    ♣ 6 4 2
    ♠ 5                              ♠ K 8 7 6
    ♡ Q J 10 9 2         N          ♡ 5 4
    ◇ K 8 5         W        E      ◇ Q J 7 6
    ♣ J 10 9 3           S          ♣ Q 8 7
                    ♠ A Q 10 4
                    ♡ K 7 6
                    ◇ A 10 9
                    ♣ A K 5
```

Holding 20 points and a fair ration of tens and nines, South opened classically with two no trumps. North's ace and jack were sufficient for a raise to three. (Note that it would be foolish for North, with 4—3—3—3 distribution, to bid a Stayman three clubs, looking for a fit in spades. He would find the fit all right, but in spades there are four inevitable losers, apart from the trump suit.)

West led the queen of hearts and South was confronted with a simple proposition: if he could pick up the king of spades there would be nine tricks—no more, no less.

Pleased to find that there were no problems, South won with the ace of hearts and put the spade finesse to the test by leading the jack from dummy. East did not oblige by covering with the king—which would, indeed, have been poor play. When the jack was not covered, South thought for a moment of unblocking the ten. Realizing eventually that this could make no difference, he played low from hand and followed with another spade, finessing the ten. When West showed out it was apparent that he would have to lose a spade to the king and would be unable to make more than eight tricks.

All that was required here was to lead the nine from dummy on the first round of spades, not the jack. Then the defence cannot prevent the declarer from winning four spade tricks.

Here are two more combinations where some care may be needed:

1) Q 9 5   2) 10 7 6

   A J 10 4   A Q J 9 2

To pick up four fast tricks when East holds K x x x, South must lead the nine from dummy in the first example. In the second example, South leads the ten from dummy and should unblock the nine from his own hand. This will enable him to run five quick tricks when West has a singleton eight.

Example 7

On the next hand South has a run of six cards in sequence from the jack to the six, but the contract still depends on which card he leads first.

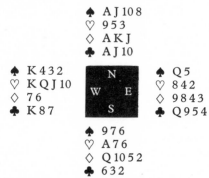

♠ A J 10 8
♡ 9 5 3
◇ A K J
♣ A J 10

♠ K 4 3 2   ♠ Q 5
♡ K Q J 10   ♡ 8 4 2
◇ 7 6   ◇ 9 8 4 3
♣ K 8 7   ♣ Q 9 5 4

♠ 9 7 6
♡ A 7 6
◇ Q 10 5 2
♣ 6 3 2

Most modern players, if not playing a strong no trump, would begin with an approach bid of one club on the North hand. The alternative is a somewhat old-fashioned one spade. South responds one no trump to one spade and North, attaching full value to his two A J 10 combinations, is well worth a raise to three no trumps.

West opens the king of hearts, and as hearts are evidently the danger suit South holds up his ace until the third round. There are seven tricks on top and a reasonably good lie of the spades will produce the extra tricks that are required. Let us say that after winning the third round of hearts South leads the nine of spades, as many players would. East wins with the queen and returns a diamond—the safest play available.

Taking care not to block the diamonds, South wins with the king in dummy, cashes the ace, and overtakes the jack with the queen. The position is then:

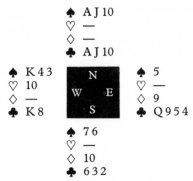

When South leads the fourth diamond West must let go the ten of hearts, while dummy throws a club. South now finesses the ten of spades. If he has read the distribution well enough to follow with the ace of clubs, he will test the defence: West must drop the king of clubs to avoid being thrown in and forced to lead another spade.

As we have seen, the end-game may be a little tricky. South has no problem at all, on the other hand, if his first play in spades is a low card towards the ten. Later on, he can advance the nine of spades and make three tricks in the suit.

Example 8

To play a hand of bridge well, a declarer must study the prospects in individual suits, then form an overall plan that takes all the elements into account.

Players are often advised to lead the highest card for a finesse when they will not mind if this card is covered. On most hands, holding 10 x x opposite A J 9 8 x, it would be in order to lead the ten; but as we have seen, the entry position may have a bearing.

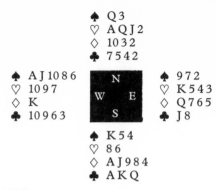

```
              ♠ Q 3
              ♡ A Q J 2
              ◊ 10 3 2
              ♣ 7 5 4 2
♠ A J 10 8 6                      ♠ 9 7 2
♡ 10 9 7          N              ♡ K 5 4 3
◊ K           W       E          ◊ Q 7 6 5
♣ 10 9 6 3        S              ♣ J 8
              ♠ K 5 4
              ♡ 8 6
              ◊ A J 9 8 4
              ♣ A K Q
```

This was the bidding:

SOUTH	WEST	NORTH	EAST
1 ◊	1 ♠	dble	pass
2NT	pass	3NT	pass
pass	pass		

North's double of one spade was of the variety known as 'sputnik'. When this convention is played, a double of intervention after partner has opened is not a penalty double but denotes moderate values in the range of about 7 to 10. This was a good hand for the convention, because no alternative would have been satisfactory. As a sputnik double of one spade will usually contain four hearts, South was able to jump in no trumps despite the absence of a heart guard.

West led the jack of spades and declarer played the queen from dummy. He was intending to finesse towards West, and by playing the queen of spades he retained, for the moment, a second guard in the suit. At trick two, declarer made the mistake of leading the ten of diamonds from dummy, letting it run to West's king.

An instructive point in defence now arose. It may seem that the natural play for West is to lead a heart through dummy's strength, but this would not be correct, though it would have made no difference as the cards lay. If South needs the heart finesse he will take it whether hearts are led now, or not. Thus there is no hurry to play hearts; when in with the king of diamonds West must lead a club, because partner may hold the ace of clubs and South the king of hearts.

Declarer won the club switch and crossed to the ace of hearts, spurning the finesse because he hoped to make four tricks in diamonds, which would be enough for game. When he led a low diamond from dummy, the eight held, but West showed out. Now South could take only seven tricks and was two down on a contract which would have been very simple if he had led a low diamond from the table at trick two instead of the ten.

Example 9

There are innumerable situations where the declarer must play in a special manner to ensure good communication. The deal below shows that there is sometimes an art in playing such an apparently simple combination as Q 10 9 opposite A J x.

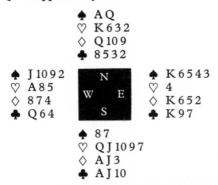

```
              ♠ A Q
              ♡ K 6 3 2
              ◇ Q 10 9
              ♣ 8 5 3 2
  ♠ J 10 9 2      N        ♠ K 6 5 4 3
  ♡ A 8 5                  ♡ 4
  ◇ 8 7 4    W      E      ◇ K 6 5 2
  ♣ Q 6 4         S        ♣ K 9 7
              ♠ 8 7
              ♡ Q J 10 9 7
              ◇ A J 3
              ♣ A J 10
```

South opens one heart, North has an obvious raise to three hearts, and South goes to four hearts. West leads the jack of spades.

The spade finesse is not likely to win, but it cannot be avoided, so declarer puts in the queen, losing to the king. Many players in East's position would lead a club up to the weakness in dummy, but it is better play to return a spade to dummy's ace. Declarer will no doubt need to play diamonds and clubs himself, and there is no point in assisting him, as he may be short of entries to the table.

In dummy with the ace of spades, declarer must use the entry to the best advantage by finessing the ten of clubs. West wins with the queen and exits with a low heart. South takes this trick and leads the queen of hearts. West plays the ace and, still giving nothing away, returns a third heart to dummy's king. The position is now:

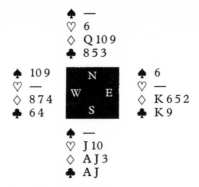

```
              ♠ —
              ♡ 6
              ◇ Q 10 9
              ♣ 8 5 3
  ♠ 10 9        N        ♠ 6
  ♡ —                    ♡ —
  ◇ 8 7 4    W     E     ◇ K 6 5 2
  ♣ 6 4         S        ♣ K 9
              ♠ —
              ♡ J 10
              ◇ A J 3
              ♣ A J
```

South is in dummy for the last time and needs to finesse against both minor suit kings. It is essential that he lead the queen of diamonds from dummy and drop the jack from hand. Then (assuming that East has not covered) he can follow with the ten of diamonds. If East plays low again, the ten will hold the trick and declarer will be able to follow with a second finesse in clubs.

If South plays the diamonds in any other way, East, by covering at the right moment, will force South to take the trick, with no entry to dummy for the club finesse.

Example 10

The top honours are pleasant to see at any time, and a bridge player soon becomes familiar with the management of aces, kings and queens. The role of the low cards is not quite so easy to appreciate. Here is a deal where a lowly deuce provided the declarer with the only means to land a slam contract.

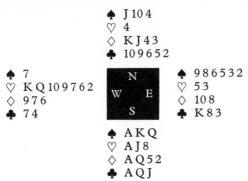

```
                    ♠ J 10 4
                    ♡ 4
                    ♢ K J 4 3
                    ♣ 10 9 6 5 2
  ♠ 7                               ♠ 9 8 6 5 3 2
  ♡ K Q 10 9 7 6 2    N            ♡ 5 3
  ♢ 9 7 6          W     E          ♢ 10 8
  ♣ 7 4                S            ♣ K 8 3
                    ♠ A K Q
                    ♡ A J 8
                    ♢ A Q 5 2
                    ♣ A Q J
```

In a pairs tournament South was the dealer and North-South were vulnerable. The bidding followed an interesting course:

SOUTH	WEST	NORTH	EAST
2 ♣	2 ♡	pass	pass
3NT	pass	4 ♣ (1)	pass
4 ♢	pass	5 ♢	pass
6 ♢	pass	pass	6 ♡ (2)
6NT (3)	pass	pass	pass

1) The sequence of two clubs, followed by three no trumps, indicated a very strong hand of 25 points or more. North showed good judgement in keeping the auction alive; if clubs did not appeal, then four no trumps would surely be safe.

2) This startling call resulted from the special conditions of pairs play. With his king of clubs a dead duck, East had little or no hope of defeating six diamonds, which would be worth 1370 to his vulnerable opponents. If the penalty in hearts could be kept to 1300 or less, he might score well on the deal. At rubber bridge it would be silly to invite such a big penalty, but in a pairs the small gain from the sacrifice might be important.

21

3) South, who had given serious thought to bidding six no trumps on the previous round, now does so. He realizes that six no trumps may not be so sound a contract as six diamonds, but he is unwilling to accept what may be an insufficient penalty. (East-West, in fact, can make six tricks in hearts; by playing diamonds and threatening to take a ruff in dummy, West can force the opposition to play trumps.)

The play in six no trumps is not difficult and may, indeed, be compared to some similar hands in our companion work, *Blocking and Unblocking Plays*. West leads the king of hearts and South has no reason to hold off. He wins with the ace, plays ace of diamonds and follows with the five of diamonds to dummy's jack. The club finesse wins and the queen of diamonds is led to dummy's king, for a second finesse in clubs. The ace of clubs is cashed and the lead of the two of diamonds provides a further entry to the table. This allows South to make the two long clubs, for a total of thirteen tricks. The score of 1470, for six no trumps made with an overtrick, is sure to be well above average in a pairs contest.

Example 11

On some hands where the declarer needs entries to the dummy he may be able to exploit the fact that the defenders cannot afford to release their controls. The point of that remark is illustrated in the following deal:

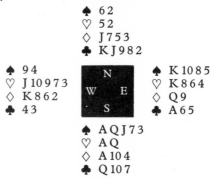

```
              ♠ 6 2
              ♡ 5 2
              ♢ J 7 5 3
              ♣ K J 9 8 2
♠ 9 4                        ♠ K 10 8 5
♡ J 10 9 7 3      N          ♡ K 8 6 4
♢ K 8 6 2      W   E         ♢ Q 9
♣ 4 3             S          ♣ A 6 5
              ♠ A Q J 7 3
              ♡ A Q
              ♢ A 10 4
              ♣ Q 10 7
```

Obviously South might open one spade, but he preferred two no trumps, which has certain tactical advantages. He has tenace holdings (that is, a combination of honours not in sequence) in all four suits, and the objection to opening one spade is that partner is very likely to respond one no trump. Then a no trump contract will be played 'the wrong way up', with the strong hand exposed and the lead coming through the high cards. One further advantage of the two no trump opening is that the defenders will not suspect the presence of a five-card major.

North raised to three no trumps and West led the jack of hearts. East played the eight; it is normally wrong to 'finesse against partner', but East was in no doubt that South held the A Q of hearts and wanted to signify to his partner that he held length in the suit.

Counting his tricks, South noted that even if he were able to establish and run the clubs he would need at least two tricks from the spades. If the defenders were able to shut out the club suit by holding up the ace, then declarer would need to rely on his second string and make four tricks in spades, together with two clubs, two hearts and one diamond.

As he might need two entries to dummy for spade finesses, South began by overtaking the ten of clubs with the jack. When East held up the ace, South took advantage of the entry to dummy by finessing the queen of spades. This was good play because, as we have seen, two spade tricks would be needed in any event.

When the queen of spades held, South led the queen of clubs, overtaking with the king. East, once again, could not afford to part with the ace. South then finessed the jack of spades and continued with ace and another. This gave him four tricks in spades. By clever management of entries he made his game contract.

Example 12

Many contracts depend on a particular card being in the hand of the right opponent. Even so, it may not be clear how to play in a manner that will give the defenders no opportunity for a counter-stroke.

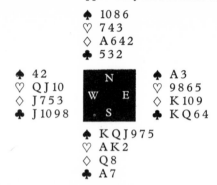

```
              ♠ 10 8 6
              ♡ 7 4 3
              ◇ A 6 4 2
              ♣ 5 3 2
  ♠ 4 2          N          ♠ A 3
  ♡ Q J 10   W       E      ♡ 9 8 6 5
  ◇ J 7 5 3               ◇ K 10 9
  ♣ J 10 9 8     S          ♣ K Q 6 4
              ♠ K Q J 9 7 5
              ♡ A K 2
              ◇ Q 8
              ♣ A 7
```

North-South were playing the Acol system, in which opening bids of two spades, two hearts and two diamonds are forcing for one round. South opened two spades and North gave the weakness response of two no trumps. Having shown a big hand already, it was sufficient for South to bid three spades. Holding an ace and some trump support, North had a sound raise to four spades.

West led the queen of hearts and South won with the ace. It seemed at first that there was a certain loser in each suit, but it occurred to South in time that if he could find East with the king of diamonds he might succeed in establishing a second trick in diamonds. On this he would be able to dispose of one of his losers, either a heart or a club.

Realizing that he would need entries to dummy for this manoeuvre, South led the king of spades from hand in the naïve expectation that this would tempt the defenders to part with the ace. East had played the game before, however, and though he could not visualize the entire hand he saw that dummy was short of entries and decided to hold up the ace of trumps. East won the second trump and exited with a heart, won by the king. The declarer now had what backgammon players call a 'nothing game'. He was able to cross to dummy on the third round of trumps and lead a diamond towards the queen, but East went up with the king on the first round, and after he had cashed the queen South was unable to cross to dummy to enjoy a trick with the ace.

The mistake was the earlier lead of the king of spades. South should have led the nine and overtaken with the ten. If East holds off, South plays a diamond from the table at once. East takes the king and returns a heart. South cashes the queen of diamonds, forces out the ace of spades, and is able to enter dummy on the third round of trumps. His losing club now goes away on the ace of diamonds.

Example 13

The next hand appears to have the same general theme as the last one: with A x x x of clubs in dummy, Q x in hand, the declarer must aim to establish an extra trick by finding East with the king. However, this example contains a trap that might well deceive an experienced player.

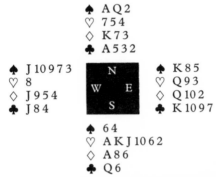

$$\begin{array}{cccc}
& \spadesuit \ \text{A Q 2} \\
& \heartsuit \ \text{7 5 4} \\
& \diamondsuit \ \text{K 7 3} \\
& \clubsuit \ \text{A 5 3 2} \\
\end{array}$$

♠ J 10 9 7 3   N   ♠ K 8 5
♡ 8   W   E   ♡ Q 9 3
◇ J 9 5 4   ◇ Q 10 2
♣ J 8 4   S   ♣ K 10 9 7

♠ 6 4
♡ A K J 10 6 2
◇ A 8 6
♣ Q 6

South opens one heart and North, with a flat 13, responds two no trumps—all that his hand is worth. With 6—3—3—2 distribution there is a good case for three no trumps on the South hand, but most players, seduced by the honours, would rebid four hearts.

Let us see how the play in hearts is likely to go after the lead of the jack of spades. Observing that there is no way to avoid a spade loser if the finesse if wrong, South tries the queen. East wins and, we will say, returns a spade. As he may wish to establish a trick in clubs for a diamond discard, South leads a low club from dummy. East wins and plays a third spade, which South ruffs.

Two rounds of trumps fail to bring down the queen, but South is able to cash the queen of clubs, concede a heart to the queen, and later discard a diamond on the ace of clubs. Four hearts made, and everyone is happy.

But both East and South have made a mistake. What were they ?

It is not altogether obvious, but when in with the king of spades East should return a diamond, not a spade. To protect his entry to the table, South goes up with the ace and draws two top trumps, as before. Having failed to bring down the queen, he enters dummy with the ace of spades and leads up to the queen of clubs. The position at this point is:

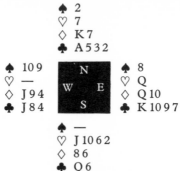

	♠ 2	
	♡ 7	
	◇ K 7	
	♣ A 5 3 2	
♠ 10 9		♠ 8
♡ —		♡ Q
◇ J 9 4		◇ Q 10
♣ J 8 4		♣ K 10 9 7
	♠ —	
	♡ J 10 6 2	
	◇ 8 6	
	♣ Q 6	

East goes up with the king of clubs, pulls the queen of hearts, and exits with a diamond. This removes the entry from dummy, and after making his queen of clubs South cannot return to cash the ace.

Thus a perfect defence appears to beat the contract, but South can do better (without the aid of a good guess in trumps). The spade finesse at trick one, allowing the defence to switch to a diamond, is a miscalculation. Declarer should go up with the ace of spades and lead a club at one. If East plays the king, then dummy's entry cannot be forced out before it is needed. And if the club lead proves a failure, South still has time to benefit from a favourable lie of the king of spades. It is a difficult hand, worth studying from both sides of the table.

Example 14

Many contracts are lost because the declarer fails to make a plan at the outset and arrives at a position from which he cannot extricate himself. One of the present authors was the sufferer when the following hand occurred:

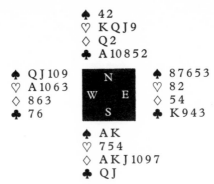

```
                    ♠ 4 2
                    ♡ K Q J 9
                    ◇ Q 2
                    ♣ A 10 8 5 2
    ♠ Q J 10 9                      ♠ 8 7 6 5 3
    ♡ A 10 6 3         N            ♡ 8 2
    ◇ 8 6 3        W       E        ◇ 5 4
    ♣ 7 6             S             ♣ K 9 4 3
                    ♠ A K
                    ♡ 7 5 4
                    ◇ A K J 10 9 7
                    ♣ Q J
```

The bidding went smoothly enough:

SOUTH	WEST	NORTH	EAST
2 ◇	pass	3 ♣	pass
3 ◇	pass	3 ♡	pass
3 NT	pass	4 ◇	pass
6 ◇	pass	pass	pass

A club lead would have given the declarer no chance, but West made the natural lead of the queen of spades. South won with the ace, drew trumps in three rounds, then led a heart to the king, which held. East played the eight, to indicate an even number. South came back to the king of spades to lead another heart.

West, meanwhile, had done a little counting. It was plain that declarer had six diamonds, two spades, two hearts and the ace of clubs in his pocket. To go up with the ace of hearts would surrender all chance of beating the contract.

When West played a low heart on the second round, South contemplated a finesse of the nine but was aware that he would look a little foolish if this lost to the ten. He went up with the queen, therefore, and having no entry back to hand played a third heart from the table. The hearts did not break and eventually South had to try the club finesse, which also proved a disappointment.

Vaguely aware that he had not distinguished himself, South explained his reasons for not finessing the nine of hearts on the second round of the suit. North, who had to finish the rubber with the same partner, observed blandly that the bidding had been splendid and the lie of the cards unfortunate.

South, of course, should have foreseen that it might be necessary to lead three times towards dummy's K Q J 9 of hearts. After just one round of trumps he should have led a heart towards the dummy, taking the very small risk of encountering a ruff. When the king holds, he returns to the ace of diamonds, draws the remaining trump, and leads a second heart. If West again plays low, South can return to the king of spades for another lead of hearts which, as the cards lie, will establish a winner for the discard of a club.

Example 15

We turn now from problems of communication to a form of play that is especially common in no trump contracts. This consists of avoiding, whenever possible, the loss of a trick to the 'danger hand'.

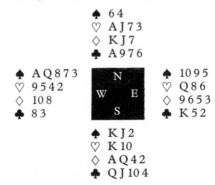

```
              ♠ 6 4
              ♡ A J 7 3
              ◇ K J 7
              ♣ A 9 7 6
♠ A Q 8 7 3                  ♠ 10 9 5
♡ 9 5 4 2        N           ♡ Q 8 6
◇ 10 8       W     E         ◇ 9 6 5 3
♣ 8 3            S           ♣ K 5 2
              ♠ K J 2
              ♡ K 10
              ◇ A Q 4 2
              ♣ Q J 10 4
```

Playing a 15—17 no trump, South opened one no trump. West passed and North responded two clubs, Stayman. When South denied possession of a major by rebidding two diamonds, North settled for three no trumps.

Players are not as faithful as they used to be to the lead of fourth best against no trumps and West on this occasion led the three of spades, a small deception that perhaps caused South to lower his guard. At any rate, he won with the jack, noting that he had eight tricks on top. The clubs seemed the most promising location for extra tricks, so he ran the jack of clubs at trick two. East won with the king and a spade return gave West four spade tricks, enough to defeat the contract.

'You open a strong no trump, I put down 13 points, and you can't make three no trumps,' remarked North a little bitterly.

It was as well for partnership morale that North did not inspect the play more closely. After the spade lead East was the danger hand, in the sense that declarer, who still had the guarded king of spades, could afford to lose a trick to West, but not to East. He should have looked, therefore, for some way of finessing into the West, not the East, hand—assuming, of course, that this finesse would be capable of producing enough tricks for the contract.

After winning the first trick with the jack of spades South should cross to dummy with a diamond and lead a low heart, finessing the ten. As the cards lie, the finesse wins. South then cashes the king of hearts, crosses to dummy with another diamond and leads the ace of hearts. When the queen falls he has an overtrick.

If the finesse of the ten of hearts loses to West, South still makes his contract with one spade, three hearts, four diamonds and a club.

Example 16

The next deal illustrates a very important principle in the play at no trumps: when there are two suits to establish, attack first the entry of the danger hand. When you play the second suit you may find that the opponents are no longer in communication.

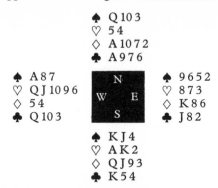

```
              ♠ Q 10 3
              ♡ 5 4
              ◇ A 10 7 2
              ♣ A 9 7 6
  ♠ A 8 7                    ♠ 9 6 5 2
  ♡ Q J 10 9 6    N          ♡ 8 7 3
  ◇ 5 4        W     E       ◇ K 8 6
  ♣ Q 10 3        S          ♣ J 8 2
              ♠ K J 4
              ♡ A K 2
              ◇ Q J 9 3
              ♣ K 5 4
```

North was the dealer and after two passes South, who was playing a 12—14 no trump not vunerable, opened one diamond. West overcalled with one heart. If he had not already passed, North might have made an approach bid of two clubs, but he did not want to risk being left in that contract, so he gave a straightforward raise to three diamonds. South naturally converted to three no trumps.

West led the queen of hearts. Following general principles, South held off the first heart, won the second, and finessed the queen of diamonds. East won and cleared the hearts.

When the diamonds were played off, West had to find three discards. The first two were easy enough—the eight and seven of spades. The last was not so easy, but West decided that if South held K J x of clubs the hand could not be defended. He let go a club, therefore, and made the ace of spades and two more hearts to defeat the contract by one trick.

South could see from the beginning that he would need at least one trick in spades, and possibly two. It was essential to attack the entry of the danger hand, West. The best line was to win the first heart and lead a spade. If the first spade is allowed to win, he must play a second round. West will probably win and lead another heart. South wins and takes the diamond finesse. East wins but has no heart to play, and West, since the ace of spades has been forced out, has no quick entry. South makes game by way of three diamonds, two spades, two hearts and two clubs.

Example 17

One of the commonest problems in the game is how to tackle a combination of eight cards, missing the queen, such as:

A 7 4

K J 6 5 2

Most players realize that, initially the queen is more likely to be in the hand with three cards rather than the hand with two, but after they have played ace and another, and the queen has not appeared, they tend to review the situation. At this moment there are only two cards outstanding and it is tempting to suppose that the card held on the left (assuming a 3—2 break) is as likely to be the queen as a low card. Thus it may seem as reasonable to play for the drop as to finesse.

There is a fallacy in this line of argument, as can readily be seen if the example is transferred to a different setting. Suppose you hold four copper coins and one silver coin and you distribute at random two coins to West and three to East. At this moment, obviously, East is more likely to hold the silver coin. Now if you demand one coin from West, two from East, stipulating always that the silver coin is not to be freely given up, the probabilities must remain the same. In short, the finesse is still the better play.

There are, nevertheless, many occasions where it is right to spurn the finesse for tactical reasons. This is a fairly simple example:

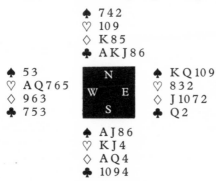

```
                    ♠ 7 4 2
                    ♡ 10 9
                    ◇ K 8 5
                    ♣ A K J 8 6
    ♠ 5 3              N              ♠ K Q 10 9
    ♡ A Q 7 6 5                       ♡ 8 3 2
    ◇ 9 6 3       W         E         ◇ J 10 7 2
    ♣ 7 5 3              S            ♣ Q 2
                    ♠ A J 8 6
                    ♡ K J 4
                    ◇ A Q 4
                    ♣ 10 9 4
```

South plays in three no trumps and West leads the six of hearts, won by dummy's ten. Clearly it would be foolish to enter hand for the club finesse, for the one thing that South must avoid is to let East in the lead to play a heart through the K J. Declarer does not mind losing to the queen of clubs in the West hand, because West can do him no damage. The right play, therefore, is to play off ace and king of clubs—with a happy result, as the cards lie.

Example 18

Three examples follow of hands in a suit contract where the declarer must be aware of the danger threatened by a particular opponent. The first hand was well bid by the North-South pair.

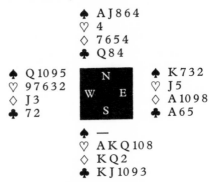

```
                    ♠ A J 8 6 4
                    ♡ 4
                    ♦ 7 6 5 4
                    ♣ Q 8 4
    ♠ Q 10 9 5                      ♠ K 7 3 2
    ♡ 9 7 6 3 2      N              ♡ J 5
    ♦ J 3         W     E           ♦ A 10 9 8
    ♣ 7 2            S              ♣ A 6 5
                    ♠ —
                    ♡ A K Q 10 8
                    ♦ K Q 2
                    ♣ K J 10 9 3
```

Playing Acol, South opened two hearts and the bidding continued:

SOUTH	WEST	NORTH	EAST
2♡	pass	2♠	pass
3♣	pass	4♣	pass
5♣	pass	pass	pass

It is a type of hand on which players have been known to reach a small slam, missing two aces. Note that it would be unsound for South to bid a Blackwood four no trumps because a response of five diamonds, if based on the ace of spades, would carry him overboard.

With no very attractive lead against five clubs, West chose the jack of diamonds. East won with the ace and returned the nine, a slightly deceptive card, because it left open the possibility that West had led from J 10 x. South realized, however, that a diamond ruff was threatened. Instead of leading a trump at once, he played off ace, king and queen of hearts, discarding two diamonds from the table. This would have averted the danger if the hearts had been 4—3, but alas, East ruffed the third heart and the declarer finished one down.

There was a safer way to avoid the diamond ruff. South should play ace of hearts, ruff a low heart and discard his master diamond, the queen, on the ace of spades. Then he can turn to clubs and deal with a diamond attack by ruffing with a high trump.

Example 19

In the last example the declarer could have prevented an adverse ruff by discarding a winner from his own hand. Sometimes it is good play to lead a high card from a combination such as K x x, so that the trick can be won only by the player who holds the ace.

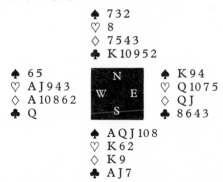

```
                    ♠ 7 3 2
                    ♡ 8
                    ◇ 7 5 4 3
                    ♣ K 10 9 5 2
        ♠ 6 5                        ♠ K 9 4
        ♡ A J 9 4 3      N           ♡ Q 10 7 5
        ◇ A 10 8 6 2   W   E         ◇ Q J
        ♣ Q              S           ♣ 8 6 4 3
                    ♠ A Q J 10 8
                    ♡ K 6 2
                    ◇ K 9
                    ♣ A J 7
```

South was the dealer with neither side vulnerable, and the bidding went:

SOUTH	WEST	NORTH	EAST
1 ♠	2 ♡	pass	3 ♡
3 ♠	4 ◇	4 ♠	pass
pass	pass		

West led his singleton queen of clubs. South won in dummy with the king, dropping the jack from hand to unblock the suit. A low spade was led to the ten, which held.

South wanted to finesse again in trumps, and clearly the safest way to enter the dummy was by ruffing a heart. South made the good play of the king of hearts from hand, forcing West to take the trick. West tried a low diamond, hoping to find his partner with the king, and South was able then to make twelve tricks by ruffing a heart, picking up the king of spades, and running the clubs.

South would probably have lost the contract if he had led a low heart at trick three instead of the king. East wins and must return, not a club, but the queen of diamonds. The defence can then take two diamond tricks, followed by a club ruff.

Example 20

On many hands the declarer has the option between a straightforward finesse through the opponent on his left or a ruffing finesse against the opponent on his right. A simple example occurs when a side suit is distributed in this fashion:

A Q J 10 4

5

Depending on the circumstances of the hand, South may seek to establish the suit by finessing the queen and ruffing the next round, or he may play the ace and take a 'ruffing finesse' against East.

A slight variation occurs when the declarer has a second card of the suit, which he is able to discard.

◇ A Q 10 9 4

◇ J 5

If able to discard a diamond, South again has the choice between a straight finesse and a ruffing finesse. That was the situation on the following deal:

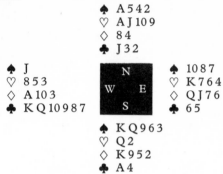

```
              ♠ A 5 4 2
              ♡ A J 10 9
              ◇ 8 4
              ♣ J 3 2
  ♠ J                        ♠ 10 8 7
  ♡ 8 5 3          N         ♡ K 7 6 4
  ◇ A 10 3      W     E      ◇ Q J 7 6
  ♣ K Q 10 9 8 7    S        ♣ 6 5
              ♠ K Q 9 6 3
              ♡ Q 2
              ◇ K 9 5 2
              ♣ A 4
```

The bidding presented no problems:

SOUTH	WEST	NORTH	EAST
1 ♠	2 ♣	3 ♠	pass
4 ♠	pass	pass	pass

West led the king of clubs and South won with the ace. As noted in our book on *Safety Plays*, the way to handle the trump suit is to lead low to the ace, so that if West happens to be void the declarer will be able to pick up East's J 10 x x. For a reason that will appear shortly, South must take care to begin with the six of spades, not the three.

As it turns out, the trumps are 3—1 and South draws them in three rounds. A heart finesse may seem to be the next move, but South has an alternative: he can play to discard a heart on the jack of clubs (which can surely be established) and then he can take a ruffing finesse against East. This will avert the danger of a lead through the king of diamonds.

After drawing trumps, therefore, South leads the four of clubs. West wins and exits with a heart. Declarer goes up with the ace, discards a heart on the jack of clubs, and leads the jack of hearts, intending to let it run if East plays low. Sooner or later, East will cover. South ruffs with the nine of spades, enters dummy by leading the carefully preserved three of spades, and cashes the remaining hearts. He makes game with five tricks in spades, three in hearts and two in clubs.

West may regret his lead of the king of clubs, but if you look at the hand again you will see that this lead made no difference. Suppose West makes a neutral lead, such as a trump. South takes an early finesse in hearts, losing to the king. When East switches to a club South goes up with the ace, draws trumps, discards one club and one diamond on the heart winners, and gives up two diamonds; there is still a trump in dummy for the other diamond loser.

Example 21

We move now to a group of hands where the declarer is concerned with establishing a long suit in dummy.

Since the days of Auction bridge there has been a popular pleasantry to the effect that there is many a man walking the Embankment because he failed to draw trumps. The conclusion that it is always right to draw trumps must be regarded with some distrust, however. The trump suit is often an important thoroughfare between declarer and dummy. We saw one example in deal No 12, and here is another:

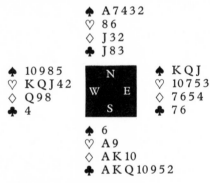

```
              ♠ A 7 4 3 2
              ♡ 8 6
              ◇ J 3 2
              ♣ J 8 3

♠ 10 9 8 5         N          ♠ K Q J
♡ K Q J 4 2    W       E      ♡ 10 7 5 3
◇ Q 9 8                       ◇ 7 6 5 4
♣ 4                 S         ♣ 7 6

              ♠ 6
              ♡ A 9
              ◇ A K 10
              ♣ A K Q 10 9 5 2
```

South was the dealer and the bidding went:

SOUTH	WEST	NORTH	EAST
2♣(1)	pass	2♠(2)	pass
3♣	pass	3♠	pass
4♣	pass	5♣	pass
6♣(3)	pass	pass	pass

1) Conventional.

2) The hand was played in France, where 'ace responses to two clubs' are popular. Thus two spades signified the ace, not a suit.

3) South finds it reasonable to hope that he will be able to dispose of one of his red-suit losers.

West led the king of hearts and South won with the ace. If he draws trumps he is thrown back on the diamond finesse as his only real hope for the contract. There is an additional chance, however—to find the spades 4—3 and the clubs 2—1.

Even one round of trumps would be an error. South must begin by leading a spade to the ace and ruffing a spade with a high trump. Then he leads the nine of clubs to the jack and ruffs another spade, again with a high trump.

By this time the declarer knows his fate. As the cards lie, both opponents follow to the third round of spades and to the first round of clubs. South plays the five of clubs to dummy's eight, ruffs a fourth round of spades, and returns with the two of clubs to dummy's three, to cash the last spade and discard a heart.

If either black suit proves disappointing, South can change his plan and finesse for the queen of diamonds.

Example 22

When the declarer is playing to establish a suit in dummy he must be careful to use entries in the right order. There was a temptation on the deal below to take a ruff in dummy too soon.

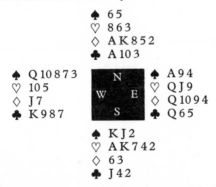

```
                    ♠ 6 5
                    ♡ 8 6 3
                    ◇ A K 8 5 2
                    ♣ A 10 3
    ♠ Q 10 8 7 3              ♠ A 9 4
    ♡ 10 5         N          ♡ Q J 9
    ◇ J 7       W     E       ◇ Q 10 9 4
    ♣ K 9 8 7      S          ♣ Q 6 5
                    ♠ K J 2
                    ♡ A K 7 4 2
                    ◇ 6 3
                    ♣ J 4 2
```

South opened with a minimum bid of one heart and the bidding continued:

SOUTH	WEST	NORTH	EAST
1 ♡	pass	2 ◇	pass
2 ♡	pass	4 ♡	pass
pass	pass		

Many players would have raised to three hearts only on the North hand, but four hearts was perfectly correct. In general, a player who has opening bid values (in this case, an A K and an ace) opposite an opening bid should want to be in game unless there is a palpable misfit. Here there was no question of a misfit, as North held three cards in the suit which South had rebid.

West led the seven of spades to his partner's ace, and East could see nothing more dynamic than to return a spade. A successful finesse of the jack would permit a club discard on the king of spades, but as it was most unlikely that the finesse would win, South went up with the king. Two rounds of hearts left one trump outstanding. South had arrived at this position:

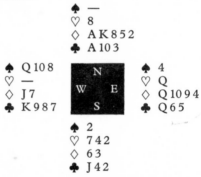

```
                    ♠ —
                    ♡ 8
                    ◇ A K 8 5 2
                    ♣ A 10 3
    ♠ Q 10 8                      ♠ 4
    ♡ —            N              ♡ Q
    ◇ J 7      W       E          ◇ Q 10 9 4
    ♣ K 9 8 7      S              ♣ Q 6 5
                    ♠ 2
                    ♡ 7 4 2
                    ◇ 6 3
                    ♣ J 4 2
```

It was important now to play the cards in the right order. Because the diamonds may break 4—2, declarer must play on this suit at once, ruffing the third round. Only then does he take the spade ruff. A fourth diamond is trumped, setting up the long diamond as a winner. South crosses to the ace of clubs and plays the good diamond, discarding a club. The defence makes only two more tricks, a trump and a club.

Example 23

To stay alive and trust to luck is an agreeable formula for many situations in life, but as a motto for bridge players it lacks iron discipline. To be afraid all the time of bad distributions makes for slow play and loss of concentration on more important matters, but when there is an obvious chance that a suit may break badly it is very necessary to examine alternative ways of making the contract. The following hand presents problems in both bidding and play:

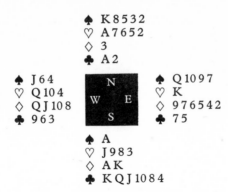

```
              ♠ K8532
              ♡ A7652
              ◇ 3
              ♣ A2
 ♠ J64                          ♠ Q1097
 ♡ Q104          N              ♡ K
 ◇ QJ108      W     E           ◇ 976542
 ♣ 963           S              ♣ 75
              ♠ A
              ♡ J983
              ◇ AK
              ♣ KQJ1084
```

It is a tricky hand to bid, because of the danger of ending in six hearts instead of six clubs. This is a possible route:

SOUTH	NORTH
1♣	1♠
3♣	3♡
4♡	5♣
6♣	pass

West leads the queen of diamonds and South wins with the ace. There are eleven tricks on top, but it would be lazy to rely on the hearts producing a twelfth trick. There are too many ways of losing two tricks in this suit before an extra trick can be developed.

The declarer should note (before drawing trumps) that it may be possible to establish the fifth round of spades. The order of play, after the ace of diamonds, is: ace of spades, club to the ace, ruff a low spade; ruff the king of diamonds (the critical move); ruff a spade with the ten of clubs. When all follow, South can see daylight, for the K 8 of spades are now good. After drawing trumps, declarer crosses to the ace of hearts and discards two hearts on the winning spades.

Oddly enough, it would be easier to perceive the right line of play if declarer held A x of diamonds instead of A K. To ruff the king of diamonds with the two of clubs is just as certain a trick as letting it ride; as we have seen, the ruff is vital for reasons of entry.

Example 24

It may not be difficult to see that there are chances to establish a suit in dummy; not difficult to count how many entries will be required; and not difficult, when the count is sufficient, to see that establishing winners is a more promising line than playing a suit where you need to find a card on the right side, with only a 50% chance of success. However, it may be difficult to 'put all this together', especially when there are alternative ways of playing the trump suit. Do not be discouraged if you do not see the best line of play immediately, while more experienced players would need only one glance at the combined hands. It is all a matter of practice and familiarity. That is why we present you with four or five hands in succession which are closely related in theme.

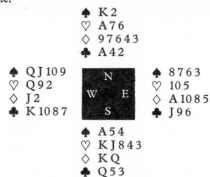

```
                    ♠ K 2
                    ♡ A 7 6
                    ◇ 9 7 6 4 3
                    ♣ A 4 2
  ♠ Q J 10 9                        ♠ 8 7 6 3
  ♡ Q 9 2                           ♡ 10 5
  ◇ J 2                             ◇ A 10 8 5
  ♣ K 10 8 7                        ♣ J 9 6
                    ♠ A 5 4
                    ♡ K J 8 4 3
                    ◇ K Q
                    ♣ Q 5 3
```

South opens one heart, North responds two diamonds, and South rebids two hearts. North raises to three hearts. (If you ask why we advise only three hearts here, while we commended the raise to four hearts on Example 22, the answer is that the present hand is less flexible. The side suit is weak and may be difficult to establish, and three low trumps, with compensating values outside, is a better holding than A x x of trumps.) South has better than a minimum opening and will go to four hearts over the raise to three.

West leads the queen of spades and declarer sees that there is a sure loser in diamonds, a possible loser in trumps, and perhaps two losers in clubs. However, if the diamonds can be established it may be possible to obtain at least one discard and not rely on the clubs to provide a second trick.

Because all dummy's entries may be needed, the first move is to win with the ace of spades and advance the king of diamonds. Say that East wins and knocks out dummy's king of spades, which is as good a defence as any: South crosses to the queen of diamonds, and all follow. At this point the contract is safe, so long as the trumps are not worse than 3—2. South must not risk a losing finesse in hearts. Instead, he plays king of hearts and a low heart to the ace. These are the remaining cards:

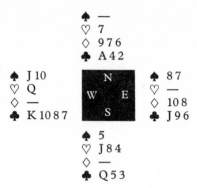

```
              ♠ —
              ♡ 7
              ◇ 9 7 6
              ♣ A 4 2
  ♠ J 10         N        ♠ 8 7
  ♡ Q       W        E    ♡ —
  ◇ —                     ◇ 10 8
  ♣ K 10 8 7      S       ♣ J 9 6
              ♠ 5
              ♡ J 8 4
              ◇ —
              ♣ Q 5 3
```

South leads a diamond and ruffs. It makes no difference whether or
not West overruffs. Suppose he does not: then declarer ruffs a spade
and plays a fourth diamond, ruffing again. The fifth diamond is good
now, for the discard of a losing club. South makes game for the loss
of one trump, one diamond and one club.

Example 25

Some hands seem to be full of finesses and it may not be obvious at
first which finesse to take and whether, instead, to attempt to
establish a long suit.

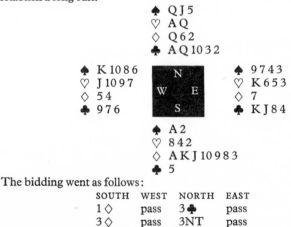

```
              ♠ Q J 5
              ♡ A Q
              ◇ Q 6 2
              ♣ A Q 10 3 2
  ♠ K 10 8 6     N        ♠ 9 7 4 3
  ♡ J 10 9 7  W       E   ♡ K 6 5 3
  ◇ 5 4                   ◇ 7
  ♣ 9 7 6        S        ♣ K J 8 4
              ♠ A 2
              ♡ 8 4 2
              ◇ A K J 10 9 8 3
              ♣ 5
```

The bidding went as follows:

SOUTH	WEST	NORTH	EAST
1 ◇	pass	3 ♣	pass
3 ◇	pass	3NT	pass
4 ◇(1)	pass	4 ♡(2)	pass
4 ♠(3)	pass	6 ◇(4)	pass
pass	pass		

1) With a hand on which he would have made a jump rebid of three diamonds over a simple response of two clubs, South is certainly going to try for a slam after partner has forced.

2) North would not be introducing a new suit at this level, so four hearts is obviously a 'cue-bid', showing a control in hearts and implying support for diamonds.

3) South responds with a cue-bid in spades.

4) Many players, with their eyes fixed on the two A Q combinations, would bid six no trumps at this point. However, North has already bid no trumps and his partner can convert if he wishes. As the play will show, the advantage of playing with a long trump suit is that this can be used for the establishment of a side suit—clubs in this case.

When the jack of hearts is led, South can see finesse positions in three suits. It may be possible to avoid the heart finesse by coming to hand with a trump, finessing the queen of clubs, and eventually establishing the fifth club for an additional discard. However, the heart finesse *may* win (West might have made an attacking lead from K J 10 through a suit where dummy is expected to hold the ace) and several other chances remain, so the natural play for declarer is to put in the queen.

East wins with the king of hearts and his obvious return is a spade. It is better play, however, to return a heart, removing an entry from the dummy before South has begun to establish the clubs. If declarer needs the spade finesse for his contract he will take it later.

In dummy with the ace of hearts, South must play immediately on clubs. He plays ace of clubs, ruffs a club high, trumps a heart with the two of diamonds, and leads a third round of clubs, again ruffing high. The position is now:

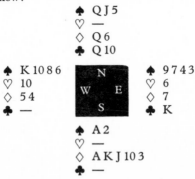

```
                ♠ Q J 5
                ♡ —
                ◇ Q 6
                ♣ Q 10
  ♠ K 10 8 6      N        ♠ 9 7 4 3
  ♡ 10       W       E     ♡ 6
  ◇ 5 4                    ◇ 7
  ♣ —            S         ♣ K
                ♠ A 2
                ♡ —
                ◇ A K J 10 3
                ♣ —
```

South has one more shot in his locker before falling back on the spade finesse. He leads the ten of diamonds to the queen, hoping to to drop the seven. When this chance succeeds he is able to ruff a club with the jack and enter dummy with the six of diamonds. A spade is thrown on the queen of clubs and the slam is made.

Example 26

When you are in a position to take a discard in one or other of two suits, consider carefully whether perhaps the discard in one suit may be worth, in effect, two tricks. This was a sad little story because South bid quite reasonably to a grand slam and then failed because he took a discard in the wrong suit.

```
                ♠  A J 10
                ♡  J 6 3 2
                ◇  J 8 7
                ♣  8 5 3
  ♠ 9 8 4 2                      ♠  7 6 5 3
  ♡ 8 7 5         N              ♡  Q 10 9
  ◇ 6 3 2     W       E          ◇  5 4
  ♣ Q 9 7         S              ♣  J 10 6 4
                ♠  K Q
                ♡  A K 4
                ◇  A K Q 10 9
                ♣  A K 2
```

South opened two clubs, intending to settle for three no trumps over the expected negative response of two diamonds. To his surprise, North replied with a positive of two no trumps, showing some values but denying a fair suit. The bidding continued:

SOUTH	NORTH
2♣	2NT
3◇	3♡(1)
4♣(2)	4◇
7◇(3)	pass

1) Not everyone's choice, but North had already denied a biddable suit and thought it would be more helpful to show that he held four hearts than to rebid three no trumps.

2) The main purpose of this bid is to see if he can wrest some diamond support from his partner, to suggest that the suit will be solid.

3) South expects his partner's hearts to be Q x x x rather than J x x x and proposes to discard his club loser on the ace of spades.

West led a trump—often best against a grand slam—and South won in hand. The only chance he could see was to discard a club on the third spade and hope to bring down the queen of hearts in two rounds. He began by playing off five rounds of diamonds, causing no great pain to the opposition. Then he took three spades, discarding a club, cashed his top clubs and hearts, and eventually conceded the thirteenth trick to the queen of hearts.

South failed to see that a 3—3 break in hearts, as well as a doubleton queen, would probably be good enough. He should draw just two rounds of trumps, leaving the jack in dummy, then play off ace and king of hearts. If the queen falls, no problem arises. If not, he discards a heart, not a club, on the third round spades, ruffs a heart with a high trump, and enters dummy with the jack of diamonds to cash the jack of hearts, which is now good. This form of play provides the solution to many contracts.

Example 27

This is a final hand on the general subject of suit establishment. The theme is the same as in the last example: the contract depends on good timing and the right choice of discards.

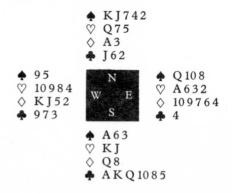

There is something to be said for opening two no trumps on the South hand, but South began with a normal one club and the bidding continued:

SOUTH	NORTH
1♣	1♠
3NT (1)	4NT (2)
6♣ (3)	pass

1) Not ideal, but it is difficult to find a better rebid. Three clubs would not express the strength.

2) Quite rightly, North gives his partner a chance to look for a slam. Four no trumps, being a raise of a natural no trump call, is 'quantitative', not Blackwood.

3) South is happy to accept the slam suggestion and sees no point in giving any further information to the opponents.

A diamond lead would have presented South with an awkward guess —whether to let it run to the queen or go up with the ace and trust the spades to provide five tricks. (If the diamond queen wins, South can play for the discard of a spade on the third heart.) However, West made the more natural lead of the ten of hearts. East won and switched to the ten of diamonds. South tried the queen without much hope, and this was covered by the king and ace. After two high trumps the position was:

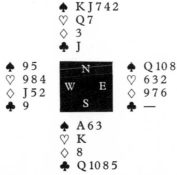

```
              ♠ K J 7 4 2
              ♡ Q 7
              ◇ 3
              ♣ J
  ♠ 9 5                      ♠ Q 10 8
  ♡ 9 8 4                    ♡ 6 3 2
  ◇ J 5 2                    ◇ 9 7 6
  ♣ 9                        ♣ —
              ♠ A 6 3
              ♡ K
              ◇ 8
              ♣ Q 10 8 5
```

Obviously South could cash the king of hearts, cross to the jack of clubs, discard a diamond on the queen of hearts, and take the spade finesse for his contract. There is a much better way, however: cash the king of hearts, play ace and king of spades, discard a *spade* on the queen of hearts, and ruff a spade with a high trump; then back to the jack of clubs to cash a long spade and dispose of the losing diamond. There are some slight risks in this play, but much less than in the simple finesse for the queen of spades.

Example 28

When a racing certainty turns up, that is the place to put your money. Sometimes the surrender of one trick ensures two others in a different suit. With that little hint, you will no doubt see the winning line on the following deal:

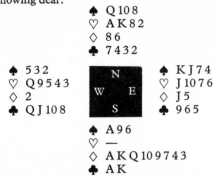

♠ Q 10 8
♡ A K 8 2
◇ 8 6
♣ 7 4 3 2

♠ 5 3 2
♡ Q 9 5 4 3
◇ 2
♣ Q J 10 8

♠ K J 7 4
♡ J 10 7 6
◇ J 5
♣ 9 6 5

♠ A 9 6
♡ —
◇ A K Q 10 9 7 4 3
♣ A K

South obviously has a game-going hand, but to open two clubs with a long diamond suit tends to lose time and may also result in the strong hand being exposed on the table. Many players prefer, therefore, to open two diamonds, forcing for one round. South did that on the hand above and the bidding continued:

SOUTH	NORTH
2 ◇	2 ♡
3 ◇ (1)	3 NT
6 ◇ (2)	pass

1) After a positive response the bidding cannot die short of game.

2) It is going to be difficult to discover whether partner has the right cards for a grand slam, and South expects to have a good play for six.

West leads the queen of clubs and South is disappointed, though not surprised, to find that his partner's main values are in hearts. There is a finesse position in spades, of course, and perhaps the jack of diamonds will fall, permitting entry to the dummy on the second round of trumps.

If South relies on one of these two chances, he will fail in the contract. The best line, after winning the first trick, is to lead a low diamond to the six. Whatever the return, South can win, cross to the eight of diamonds, and discard two spades on the ace and king of hearts.

Note that it would not matter if the diamonds were 3—0: there would still be a trump entry to the table.

Example 29

It is one of the lesser ironies of the game that extremely strong hands, when they do come along, tend to be difficult to bid with any exactness. Some tournament players, it is true, have conventional sequences at their disposal which enable them to inquire about specific cards, but in the absence of such methods (which have their drawbacks, too) it often may not be easy to discover whether partner has a particular king or queen.

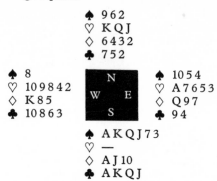

```
                    ♠ 9 6 2
                    ♡ K Q J
                    ◇ 6 4 3 2
                    ♣ 7 5 2
    ♠ 8                          ♠ 10 5 4
    ♡ 10 9 8 4 2        N        ♡ A 7 6 5 3
    ◇ K 8 5         W     E      ◇ Q 9 7
    ♣ 10 8 6 3         S         ♣ 9 4
                    ♠ A K Q J 7 3
                    ♡ —
                    ◇ A J 10
                    ♣ A K Q J
```

For South, the 'interesting' cards are the king and queen of diamonds. He bid his hand quite intelligently.

SOUTH	NORTH
2♣	2◇
2♠	2NT
3♠	4♠
5♣	5♡(1)
6♠(2)	pass

1) So far, North has shown nothing, so he is fully justified in indicating that he has some high cards in hearts.

2) South would have preferred to hear five diamonds, suggesting the king of that suit. But perhaps partner has the queen of diamonds or the ace of hearts and an entry in the trump suit. . . Even a diamond lead would be enough.

West led the ten of hearts against six spades, East played the ace and South ruffed low. Two rounds of trumps failed to drop the ten. South then laid a small trap for the opposition by playing off his top clubs. This was the situation when the third club was led:

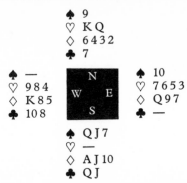

```
              ♠ 9
              ♡ K Q
              ◇ 6 4 3 2
              ♣ 7
  ♠ —            N          ♠ 10
  ♡ 9 8 4     W     E       ♡ 7 6 5 3
  ◇ K 8 5        S          ◇ Q 9 7
  ♣ 10 8                    ♣ —
              ♠ Q J 7
              ♡ —
              ◇ A J 10
              ♣ Q J
```

If East pounces on the queen of clubs with the ten of spades he presents South with the contract. East paused to reflect, however, that declarer could easily have drawn the outstanding trump and presumably had some reason for not doing so. He therefore discarded a heart on the queen of clubs and another heart on the jack of clubs. South had one more idea: he drew the trump and followed with ace and jack of diamonds: if either opponent had held a doubleton K x or Q x he would have been forced to concede a heart trick to the dummy (or vainly to drop his high card under the ace.) As it was, the defence made two diamond tricks to defeat the contract.

South made a slight error on the first trick. He should ruff the ace of hearts with the jack of spades. When the eight of spades falls under the ace he can follow with a low spade to dummy's six. Then the nine of spades will be an entry for the discard of two diamonds on the king-queen of hearts.

Example 30

When a suit is led of which the dummy is void, it is tempting to ruff, especially when there is an abundance of trumps on the table. Yet it is often better to let the lead pass, obtaining two valuable discards in return for the one loser. This hand is an example:

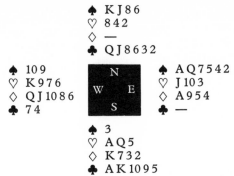

The bidding goes:

SOUTH	WEST	NORTH	EAST
1♣	pass	1♠	pass(1)
2♦	pass	4♣	pass
4♡(2)	pass	5♣	pass
pass	pass		

1) There is nothing else that East can do for the moment. To double one spade would imply length in the unbid suits, not in spades.

2) Having made a reverse bid of two diamonds, South has not much in reserve, but his partner might be stronger and anxious to hear about the heart control.

When West leads the queen of diamonds South may think that with so many trumps to spare on the table there is no reason to give up a trick to the ace of diamonds. Certainly, there are many other chances in the hand. If the heart finesse is right, only one heart and one spade will be lost; the ace of diamonds may come down in three rounds, allowing declarer to discard a heart from dummy on the king of diamonds; and a lead towards the K J 8 6 of spades may establish a spade trick in one way or another.

However, certainties are better than hopes, and declarer can make a
virtual certainty of this contract by discarding a heart from dummy
on the diamond lead. East wins with the ace and returns the jack of
hearts. South goes up with the ace, draws trumps, and discards the
last heart from dummy on the king of diamonds. He loses at most one
diamond and one spade.

It is interesting to consider what might have happened to this contract
had West made the neutral lead of a club. Declarer would draw
trumps and lead a spade, covered by the nine, jack and queen. East
returns the jack of hearts. The finesse loses, but South may later
establish a trick in spades by leading the king from dummy and
pinning West's ten.

Example 31

The deal below may appear at first to belong to the type we
considered earlier, where the choice of which suit to attack at no
trumps was of first importance. There is indeed a resemblance, but
also a new point arises.

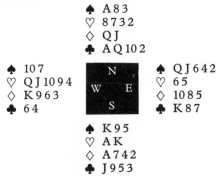

```
                    ♠ A 8 3
                    ♡ 8 7 3 2
                    ◇ Q J
                    ♣ A Q 10 2
    ♠ 10 7                          ♠ Q J 6 4 2
    ♡ Q J 10 9 4      N             ♡ 6 5
    ◇ K 9 6 3     W       E         ◇ 10 8 5
    ♣ 6 4             S             ♣ K 8 7
                    ♠ K 9 5
                    ♡ A K
                    ◇ A 7 4 2
                    ♣ J 9 5 3
```

South did not like the look of his hand for one no trump, so he
opened one diamond and the bidding continued:

SOUTH	WEST	NORTH	EAST
1 ◇	pass	2 ♣ (1)	pass
2 NT (2)	pass	3 NT	pass
pass	pass		

1) Some players consider that to by-pass a four-card major at the one level amounts to breach of promise. Since these players often end up in a totally inadequate trump suit, the style is certainly not recommended for comparatively inexperienced players.

2) A raise to three clubs would not be a mistake, but as he has a guard in both unbid suits and 15 points, South makes the more constructive rebid.

West leads the queen of hearts and South, perforce, wins with the king. What next ? Attack the danger hand—play on diamonds, not clubs ? Quite so, you have absorbed the lesson from earlier examples.

So you cross to the ace of spades and run the queen of diamonds. West wins but meanly does not persist with hearts. Realizing that his own hand is dead, he plays a second spade. East covers the ten with the jack, and the upshot is that when the club finesse loses you find that the defence has taken three spades, a diamond and a club.

This game is not easy, you are thinking. That is so, but you gave the opposition a chance by crossing to dummy for the diamond finesse, which you were fully prepared to lose. After winning the first heart you must play a low diamond from hand. Now nothing can happen to you. West takes his king of diamonds, but in due course you make two spades, two hearts, two diamonds and three clubs.

Example 32

When bridge players are talking about a hand they often use the word 'tempo'. 'The defence had the tempo', 'declarer lost a tempo', and so forth. They are speaking of the time factor—the need to make a certain play before the opposition can prepare a counterstroke. The deal above, No 31, was an example of a lost tempo (crossing to dummy for the diamond finesse). So that you will fully understand the point, here is another hand of the same type:

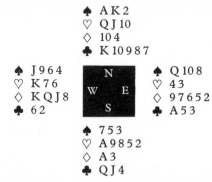

```
              ♠ A K 2
              ♡ Q J 10
              ◇ 10 4
              ♣ K 10 9 8 7
♠ J 9 6 4                      ♠ Q 10 8
♡ K 7 6                        ♡ 4 3
◇ K Q J 8                      ◇ 9 7 6 5 2
♣ 6 2                          ♣ A 5 3
              ♠ 7 5 3
              ♡ A 9 8 5 2
              ◇ A 3
              ♣ Q J 4
```

North opens one club, South responds one heart, and North raises to two hearts. Applying the test we mentioned earlier, South goes to four hearts. He has almost the values for an opening bid, facing an opening bid, and there is evidently a fit in two suits.

West leads the king of diamonds. With this type of holding, A x opposite x x, it is often right to hold off the first lead, to limit communication between the defending hands. That would be a mistake here, because West might switch to spades. South wins with the ace of diamonds, therefore.

There are certain losers in diamonds and clubs, possibly one in hearts and one in spades. South may think it sensible to cross to the ace of spades for a heart finesse. But this loses, West plays a second spade, and when East comes in with the ace of clubs he cashes a spade, the fourth trick for the defence.

After the opening lead South has the tempo, in the sense that he has time to establish both hearts and clubs before the enemy can establish a trick in spades. He can afford to lose a heart, a diamond and a club, and must not give the opponents a chance to make a spade as well.

The right play is quite obvious, therefore. South plays a low heart at trick two (better than ace and another, which may lead to entry problems if an opponent holds K x x x). The defenders may take their heart trick and attack spades, but then South can draw trumps and knock out the ace of clubs while he still has a spade control in dummy.

Example 33

When playing a contract of three no trumps, it is certainly normal to set about developing tricks in the longest suit held by the partnership. However, it is unwise to do this without considering all the circumstances of the deal. It may, as we have seen, be necessary to attack the entries of a particular hand; or it may be that declarer cannot afford to give up a trick in a suit where he has 'tops' and must play instead on a suit where the opponents already have quick winners.

Suppose, for example, that one suit consists of A K J x x opposite x x x, another of Q J 10 x x opposite x x x. If you play on the stronger suit you will probably lose one trick in this suit, plus two in the other, and furthermore your total of winners will be fewer than if you knock out ace and king of the weaker suit. Here is a more striking example of that principle:

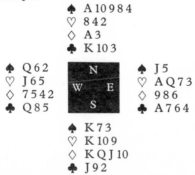

```
                    ♠ A 10 9 8 4
                    ♡ 8 4 2
                    ◇ A 3
                    ♣ K 10 3
  ♠ Q 6 2              N        ♠ J 5
  ♡ J 6 5                       ♡ A Q 7 3
  ◇ 7 5 4 2       W       E     ◇ 9 8 6
  ♣ Q 8 5              S        ♣ A 7 6 4
                    ♠ K 7 3
                    ♡ K 10 9
                    ◇ K Q J 10
                    ♣ J 9 2
```

South opens one diamond, North responds one spade, and South bids one no trump. With 11 points, a 5-card suit and good 'fillers', North is worth a raise to three no trumps.

West has a delicate choice of lead. The spades and diamonds are certainly not attractive after they have been bid by the opposition. The clubs are slightly stronger than the hearts, but when the decision is close it is usually right to attack the major suit, on the grounds that if either opponent had held this suit at all strongly he might have mentioned it. West leads the five of hearts, therefore.

With A Q x or A Q x x of a suit led by partner against no trumps it is correct to play the queen, mainly because this makes it more difficult for the declarer to hold up the king.

South captures the queen of hearts with the king and notes that he now has seven top winners. The spades are certainly the most likely source of extra tricks, but there is a very good reason not to play on spades: if South gives up a spade he will surely lose at least three hearts, a spade and a club.

A finesse against the queen of clubs, on the other hand, will bring in nine tricks if it succeeds and if the opponents can take only three tricks in hearts. It is correct to take the four diamond tricks first and then to run the nine of clubs. East will win the first or second club and, by underleading his ace, can take three heart tricks, but that is all. South still has the king of spades as an entry if he needs to take another finesse in clubs.

Example 34

The last hand showed that it is not necessarily the longest suit that must be established at no trumps. The next one shows that, as between two suits of equal length, it is not necessarily right to play on the stronger.

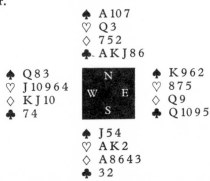

```
                    ♠ A 10 7
                    ♡ Q 3
                    ♦ 7 5 2
                    ♣ A K J 8 6
    ♠ Q 8 3                       ♠ K 9 6 2
    ♡ J 10 9 6 4        N         ♡ 8 7 5
    ♦ K J 10        W     E       ♦ Q 9
    ♣ 7 4               S         ♣ Q 10 9 5
                    ♠ J 5 4
                    ♡ A K 2
                    ♦ A 8 6 4 3
                    ♣ 3 2
```

With North the dealer at love all, the bidding goes:

SOUTH	WEST	NORTH	EAST
—	—	1 ♣	pass
1 ♢	pass	2 ♣(1)	pass
3NT(2)	pass	pass	pass

1) Some players would rebid one no trump, but others (those who play a 12—14 opening no trump) reserve this rebid for a slightly stronger hand.

2) Applying the test of opening bid facing an opening bid, South must bid game.

West leads the jack of hearts and the problem is, which suit to develop, clubs or diamonds ?

Declarer has seven top tricks and so needs to develop two extra tricks in the minor suits. There are several factors to consider.

Firstly, which suit offers the better mathematical chance ? Here a knowledge of the odds is useful. The diamonds will produce two extra tricks if they break 3—2. This is a 68% chance—better than 2 to 1 on. The clubs will produce four tricks if the suit breaks 3—3 or if they are 4—2 and the finesse for the queen is right. (You cannot count the situation where East has a doubleton queen, because you are intending to finesse the jack.) These two possibilities combined add up to about 60% ; so, a little surprisingly perhaps, there is a better chance to develop extra tricks in diamonds than in clubs.

Next, declarer must study the possible dangers. Can he afford to lose two diamonds in the process of establishing this suit ? The answer is yes. Even after the lead he has two more stoppers in hearts and the spades are reasonably safe against attack.

What about entries ? All right, because by winning the first trick in dummy and ducking twice, declarer can retain an entry in the shape of the ace of diamonds.

Finally, there is what problem-setters sometimes call the 'echelon factor'. This means, if you test one suit and it goes badly, can you fall back on the other ? Here, if the diamonds turn out to be 4—1, you still have the chance of finding the clubs 3—3, with the queen well placed. Thus again it is better to play on diamonds.

The sequence of play is: win with queen of hearts, duck a diamond; win the heart continuation, duck another diamond. When both opponents follow to this trick you know that the diamonds are established and you have enough tricks for game.

Example 35

It is a common observation among bridge players that good players seem to be lucky—not necessarily as card-holders, but in the play. Their finesses seem to work well, people seem to play badly against them.

Of course, that is largely the result of good technique. To take a very common situation, suppose you need to make a trick from the combination of K J opposite x x x. If you play this suit early on, before you know anything about the opposing hands, you have only a 50% chance of success. It is almost always possible to improve on those odds, either by obtaining information that will help you to place the cards, by discovering some additional chance that will render the finesse unnecessary, or by some technical manoeuvre that will force opponents to play towards the K J combination.

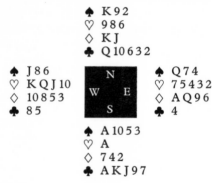

```
                        ♠ K92
                        ♡ 986
                        ◇ KJ
                        ♣ Q10632
        ♠ J86             N          ♠ Q74
        ♡ KQJ10     W         E      ♡ 75432
        ◇ 10853                      ◇ AQ96
        ♣ 85             S           ♣ 4
                        ♠ A1053
                        ♡ A
                        ◇ 742
                        ♣ AKJ97
```

The bidding goes:

SOUTH	WEST	NORTH	EAST
1♣	pass	3♣	pass
3♠	pass	4♣	pass
5♣	pass	pass	pass

A diamond lead would sink the ship, but West's natural opening is the king of hearts. South must expect to lose a spade and his problem is to avoid the loss of two diamonds.

Declarer begins by noting that West appears to have K Q, possibly K Q J, of hearts. Already there are slight grounds for placing East rather than West with the ace of diamonds. South will remember this if eventually he has to take the finesse.

Meanwhile, a favourable break in spades may allow South to discard a diamond from dummy on the fourth round of spades. After drawing trumps, declarer can lead a low spade to the nine; clearly he wants to duck this trick towards East, so that a diamond cannot be led through the K J before the spades have been tested. (If instead South were to play off ace and king of spades, a good player in East's position would throw his queen on the second round).

As the cards lie, ducking a spade towards East wins the contract. There is an even stronger line, however. Win with ace of hearts, play a club to the queen, ruff a heart; play a club to the ten, ruff a heart. Then lead ace of spades, followed by a low spade, putting in the nine from dummy. If East began with J x or Q x he will win this trick but will be left with the alternative of opening up the diamonds or leading a heart, which will allow South to ruff with his last trump while discarding a diamond from dummy. We will not dwell on this play because our companion book, *Elimination Play*, is entirely devoted to this form of technique, which has many variations.

Example 36

One of the most useful functions of aces and kings is to decapitate the opponents' kings and queens; but looking at it from the other side, there are many ways in which declarer can protect his high cards from the axe. Observe South's management of the club suit on the following deal:

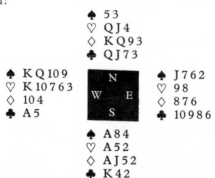

```
              ♠ 5 3
              ♡ Q J 4
              ◇ K Q 9 3
              ♣ Q J 7 3
♠ K Q 10 9         N        ♠ J 7 6 2
♡ K 10 7 6 3               ♡ 9 8
◇ 10 4       W       E     ◇ 8 7 6
♣ A 5             S        ♣ 10 9 8 6
              ♠ A 8 4
              ♡ A 5 2
              ◇ A J 5 2
              ♣ K 4 2
```

South opens one no trumps and is raised to three no trumps.

West's longest suit is hearts, but spades look the better proposition and he begins with the king, on which East shows encouragement by playing the seven. As the spades may be 5—3, with East holding the ace of clubs, declarer holds off. West continues with the queen of spades, South holds up again, and the ten of spades then forces the ace.

Clearly South must establish tricks in clubs. He begins with a low club (not the king), and dummy's queen holds the trick. This is the critical point of the deal. If South follows with a low club to the king and ace he will never come to a ninth trick, as East's 10 9 of clubs will represent a second stopper for the defence.

Unfortunate ? Not at all. It costs South nothing to return to the ace of diamonds and lead the next club from hand. West's ace then beats the air, and when the spades are seen to be 4—4 South can claim the contract.

There are several situations of this sort, where the declarer can play in a particular fashion to preserve his high cards from being axed. Here are some examples:

Q 10 7 4

K 5   A 9 8 3

J 6 2

Needing to develop two tricks, South should begin by leading low towards the hand that contains two honours. Thus on the first round of the suit the ten loses to the ace. Declarer must contrive to make the next lead also from hand, advancing the six. Now West has to play the king, and the queen and jack make separately.

This position is less well known:

J 10 7 4 3

Q 9 6 2   K 8

A 5

Aiming to establish this suit at no trumps, declarer begins with ace and another. When West plays low, declarer's best chance is to play low from dummy, not the ten or jack; if the suit breaks 3—3, the play makes no difference.

Even experienced players tend to go wrong with this combination:

5

Q 6   A 9 8 4

K J 10 7 3 2

Needing to develop the suit for the loss of two tricks, declarer leads from dummy and East plays low. The correct play is to go up with the king and return a low card. This gains when West has Q x and, as compared with finessing the ten, never loses.

Example 37

We have studied some examples of suit establishment where the declarer has to decide on which suit to stake his fortune. The next hand is a little more complicated, because the correct play, in certain circumstances, involves switching from one suit to the other.

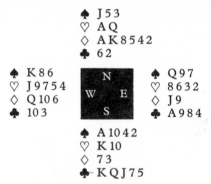

```
                    ♠ J 5 3
                    ♡ A Q
                    ◇ A K 8 5 4 2
                    ♣ 6 2
    ♠ K 8 6                        ♠ Q 9 7
    ♡ J 9 7 5 4         N          ♡ 8 6 3 2
    ◇ Q 10 6        W       E      ◇ J 9
    ♣ 10 3              S          ♣ A 9 8 4
                    ♠ A 10 4 2
                    ♡ K 10
                    ◇ 7 3
                    ♣ K Q J 7 5
```

North is the dealer and the bidding goes:

SOUTH	WEST	NORTH	EAST
—	—	1 ◇	pass
2 ♣	pass	2 ◇	pass
3 NT	pass	pass	pass

It would not be a mistake for South to bid two spades on the second round, but there are also good reasons for preferring three no trumps. In many cases it would be advantageous for the lead to come up to the K 10 of hearts—if partner held Q x x, for example, or A 9 x. Apart from that, opponents don't always lead the most dangerous suit—unless you tell them where your weakness lies.

West leads the five of hearts and the hand is bedevilled by the duplication in that suit—A Q opposite K 10 alone. The question is whether to play on diamonds or clubs or possibly on both.

Counting his tricks, declarer notes that to make five tricks in diamonds will not be enough by itself. Four tricks in clubs will be enough, however.

So far, it seems logical to play on the clubs, despite the fact that a 3—3 break in clubs is a good deal less likely than a 3—2 break in diamonds. But there is something else to consider: if declarer can snatch one club trick he can turn to diamonds, for five diamonds, two hearts, one spade and one club will be enough for game.

It may well be that the defenders cannot *afford* to take the ace of clubs on the first round. That is the situation in the present case. Declarer wins the first trick in dummy with the queen of hearts and leads a low club. East is on the spot: if he goes up with the ace he establishes four club winners, so his best play is to duck.

When South wins with the king of clubs he does not pursue this suit, nor does he duck a round of diamonds. Exploiting the echelon factor (see Example 34), he plays off ace and king of diamonds. When he sees that the diamonds are breaking he gives up the third round and has the ace of hearts for entry. If the diamonds turn out to be 4—1 he can revert to clubs, trusting that this suit will break 3—3.

Example 38

Turning now from problems of suit establishment at no trumps, we conclude with three examples of technique in suit play. In each case an average player might lose the contract without realizing that his play had been imperfect.

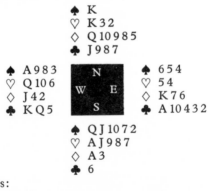

```
              ♠ K
              ♡ K 3 2
              ◇ Q 10 9 8 5
              ♣ J 9 8 7
  ♠ A 9 8 3      N        ♠ 6 5 4
  ♡ Q 10 6    W     E     ♡ 5 4
  ◇ J 4 2       S        ◇ K 7 6
  ♣ K Q 5               ♣ A 10 4 3 2
              ♠ Q J 10 7 2
              ♡ A J 9 8 7
              ◇ A 3
              ♣ 6
```

The bidding goes:

SOUTH	WEST	NORTH	EAST
1♠	pass	1NT	pass
2♡	pass	3♡	pass
4♡	pass	pass	

West leads the king of clubs and continues with the queen, South ruffing. Without giving the matter deep thought at this point, declarer leads a spade, as obviously the ace must be conceded sooner or later. West wins and plays another club, reducing the declarer to three trumps. With these cards remaining, South does not seem to be too well placed:

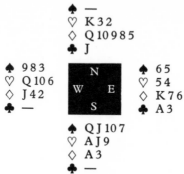

```
                    ♠ —
                    ♡ K 3 2
                    ◇ Q 10 9 8 5
                    ♣ J
    ♠ 9 8 3         ┌─────────┐      ♠ 6 5
    ♡ Q 10 6        │    N    │      ♡ 5 4
    ◇ J 4 2         │ W     E │      ◇ K 7 6
    ♣ —             │    S    │      ♣ A 3
                    └─────────┘
                    ♠ Q J 10 7
                    ♡ A J 9
                    ◇ A 3
                    ♣ —
```

Two tricks have been lost already, and as it seems that a diamond must be lost also, South may think that his best chance is to find the heart queen. He plays a heart to the king and finesses on the way back. So long as West does not commit the folly of opening up the diamonds, the defence will take another trick.

If South plays the hand in this fashion he has had a blind spot. All he needs, in the diagram position, is to find the hearts 3—2 and the spades 4—3. Keeping a tempo ahead, he draws two rounds of trumps with the king and ace, then plays off the spades, discarding four diamonds from the table. West can make the master trump when he likes, but that is all, as declarer's diamond loser can be ruffed.

With this holding of Q 10 x x opposite A x, it is easy to overlook that it may be possible to dispose of four losers in dummy.

Example 39

One of the most important skills in the game is to protect a master card from being ruffed. Suppose that in a trump contract you have a side suit of this nature:

K 7 4 2

Q led

A 9 3

Now it is possible that West's lead of the queen is a singleton, but much more likely that if there is a singleton anywhere it will be held by East. If you are not in a position to draw all the trumps immediately, it is important to win the first trick with dummy's king and not with the ace in your own hand. Then if West wins an early trick and leads the jack of his first suit, at least the king will not be ruffed.

The same principle arises here, though in a very different setting:

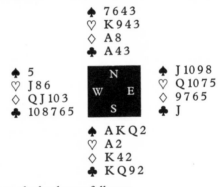

```
              ♠ 7 6 4 3
              ♡ K 9 4 3
              ◇ A 8
              ♣ A 4 3
♠ 5                        ♠ J 10 9 8
♡ J 8 6       N            ♡ Q 10 7 5
◇ Q J 10 3  W   E          ◇ 9 7 6 5
♣ 10 8 7 6 5    S          ♣ J
              ♠ A K Q 2
              ♡ A 2
              ◇ K 4 2
              ♣ K Q 9 2
```

North-South reached a slam as follows:

SOUTH	NORTH
1 ♣	1 ♡
1 ♠	3 ♠
4 NT	5 ♡
6 ♠	pass

West led the queen of diamonds and South won with the king in his own hand. There would be no problem if spades were 3—2, so declarer began by laying down the ace and the king of spades. On the second round West showed out.

South could afford to lose a trump trick so long as he could take care of the third round of diamonds and the fourth round of clubs. Tackling the clubs first, he led the king from hand, then low to the ace. Boom! East ruffed and played his last trump, leaving South with two losers to ruff and only one trump in dummy.

Let us look again at the situation after West has discarded on the second round of trumps.

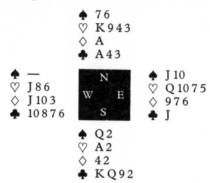

```
                    ♠ 7 6
                    ♡ K 9 4 3
                    ♢ A
                    ♣ A 4 3
        ♠ —                         ♠ J 10
        ♡ J 8 6        N            ♡ Q 10 7 5
        ♢ J 10 3    W     E         ♢ 9 7 6
        ♣ 10 8 7 6      S           ♣ J
                    ♠ Q 2
                    ♡ A 2
                    ♢ 4 2
                    ♣ K Q 9 2
```

At all costs, South must protect his high clubs from being ruffed. Instead of playing king and ace, he must begin by leading low to the ace. He cashes the ace of diamonds and leads a club to the king.

It will not help East to ruff with a good trump, so he discards. South wins, ruffs a diamond, and leads another club from dummy. If East discards again, South wins with the queen and leads his last club. East may overruff the dummy, but this will be his only trick.

Example 40

In conclusion, here is a deal where one of the authors, sitting West, played a tricky game both in the bidding and play, but to no avail.

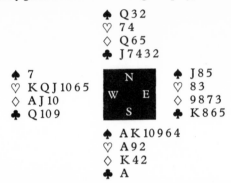

```
            ♠ Q 3 2
            ♡ 7 4
            ◇ Q 6 5
            ♣ J 7 4 3 2
  ♠ 7                      ♠ J 8 5
  ♡ K Q J 10 6 5   N       ♡ 8 3
  ◇ A J 10       W   E     ◇ 9 8 7 3
  ♣ Q 10 9         S       ♣ K 8 6 5
            ♠ A K 10 9 6 4
            ♡ A 9 2
            ◇ K 4 2
            ♣ A
```

South opened two spades and West began his campaign by passing. It would not have been particularly dangerous to overcall with three hearts, but as South had called the superior suit it was unlikely that West would be able to buy the contract at a reasonable level. Keeping silent on a strong hand sometimes produces an unusual effect.

North responded two no trumps, South bid three spades, and North raised to four spades.

When a defender can judge that the fate of the contract is likely to lie in his own hand, since he holds the majority of the cards, he may false-card, taking the view that it will not matter if his partner is misled. Acting on this principle, West led the jack of hearts. South won with the ace and, judging that he would probably need to ruff a heart, returned the nine.

West captured this with the ten and played a third heart—the five. Clearly it would be dangerous to ruff with the queen, as this might establish a trump trick for the defenders. Most players would have ruffed low and sustained an overruff. After some thought, however, South made the fine play of discarding a diamond from dummy. He later ruffed a diamond and lost only three tricks.

'I thought you might be up to something in the heart suit', said South to his opponent. Sometimes it doesn't pay to have a reputation!